Contents

KU-018-273

Contents

3604814282

A Brief Guide to Gender Statistics

In response to the Fourth United Nations World Conference on Women held in Beijing in September 1995, the Office for National Statistics and the Equal Opportunities Commission formed a partnership to take forward new projects on gender statistics. The first of these is this *Brief Guide to Gender Statistics.*

The *Guide* aims to indicate the main sources of statistics on gender-related topics for the United Kingdom and includes both official and non-government sources. It is not intended to be a comprehensive reference work and is aimed primarily at those who need to use statistics on gender-related topics but who may not have detailed specialist knowledge of statistical sources. Such users may be initially interested in statistics available in published analyses, so most references are to publications. However, for those wishing to look further, electronic datasets and databases are also referred to where appropriate. Guidance on further sources of information is contained in Section 3.

The *Guide* has four sections: a brief discussion of the main official and non-official data sources by broad topic area; a listing of the main sources of data in alphabetical order; guidance and contacts for further information; and finally, an index of topics (or keywords), cross-referring to the data sources described in Sections 1 and 2.

If you have any comments on this *Brief Guide to Gender Statistics,* please contact Magdalen Williams, Office for National Statistics, B2/11, 1 Drummond Gate, London SW1V 2QQ.

Telephone: 0171 533 5786. E-mail: magdalen.williams@ons.gov.uk.

Section 1: Gender-related statistics by theme

Gender-related statistics by theme

This section provides a general discussion of each theme in order to indicate broadly what gender data are available, which sources provide the best information and what gaps exist. Details of existing sources are given in Section 2 of the Guide.

1. General sources of gender statistics

There are several publications in which statistics are brought together to provide comparisons between women and men, either as simple summaries or as part of wider-ranging compendia. Recent examples include the *Facts about Women and Men 1997* statistics cards, the series of *Briefings on Women and Men in Britain,* and, for Northern Ireland, the statistics report *Equality Now and Then.* For international comparisons, Eurostat, the statistical office of the European Union, has published *Women and Men in the European Union.* More general compendia of statistics also draw on a range of data sources to illustrate current issues and changes over time. Perhaps the best known are the publications *Social Trends* and *Regional Trends.*

In addition, the *Social Focus* series was introduced in 1994 to describe particular groups in society. Editions so far include *Social Focus on Women, Social Focus on Families, Social Focus on Ethnic Minorities* and *Social Focus on Children,* all of which contain statistics disaggregated by gender. A range of statistics on the over-60s is presented and discussed in *Getting Around After 60,* while *Ethnic Minorities in Britain* reports on a major study on ethnicity. *Social Focus on Women and Men* and *A Statistical Focus on Wales: Women* are planned for 1998, by the Office for National Statistics and the Equal Opportunities Commission, and the Welsh Office respectively.

2. Population, households and families

The most comprehensive sources of population statistics are administrative data from the registration of births, marriages, divorces and deaths and also the *Census of Population*. Analyses of registration data plus the mid-year population estimates are published in *Population Trends*, together with patterns and trends in family formation and dissolution. Information on immigration to the United Kingdom is published in *Control of Immigration: Statistics United Kingdom*. These are all available disaggregated by gender.

The *Census of Population* provides 10-yearly benchmark figures for demographic variables at detailed geographical levels. Many census-based publications are produced, on both demographic and socio-economic topics, and samples of anonymised records from the *Census of Population 1991* are available for further analysis. Tables from the full census database can also be commissioned. *Ethnic Minority Women and the Labour Market: Analysis of the 1991 Census* is one example of the many publications based on the *Census of Population 1991* data.

The composition of households and families is recorded by regular household-based surveys such as the *General Household Survey* for Britain and the *Continuous Household Survey* for Northern Ireland. For example, statistics are available on the number of people living alone, in couples and in families with dependent children. Recent developments have included the recognition of same-sex couples as a family type.

The *British Household Panel Survey* and *Family and Working Lives Survey*, together with three birth cohort studies (the *British Cohort Study 1970, National Child Development Study* and *MRC National Survey of Health and Development*) and the census-linked *Longitudinal Study*, provide valuable research resources which track individuals and/or households over time or collect retrospective data on events.

3. Education, training and qualifications

A range of administrative data is collected by schools, colleges, local government, examination boards and employers on the education process and acquisition of qualifications. Regular and *ad hoc* surveys of individuals, educational establishments and households also collect data on past and present education, training and qualifications.

Several publications are dedicated to illustrating gender differences in education and training. *Separate Tables* contains a wide range of information, while the *Briefings on Women and Men in Britain* series provides summary information on education and vocational training in England and Wales, and in Scotland.

It can be difficult to find comparable statistics on education and training for the United Kingdom as a whole, or to combine information to obtain national estimates, because of differences in the education systems. The main annual publication which does attempt to provide consistent UK-wide national statistics is *Education Statistics for the United Kingdom,* which contains a large amount of data disaggregated by gender. The *Labour Force Survey* also provides detailed current information on education and training across the United Kingdom as a whole, while the *Youth Cohort Study* provides data on young people in England and Wales and the *Scottish School Leavers Survey* on those in Scotland. Training statistics disaggregated by gender are published in the *Labour Force Survey Quarterly Bulletin, Labour Market Trends* and *Training Statistics. The British Adult Literacy Survey* provides gender data on a broad range of related skills.

4. Labour market

Statistics on the labour market are available from surveys of households and employers, and also from administrative sources. The *Labour Force Survey* is the major household-based survey recording labour market data. This survey provides high-quality information using international definitions of economic activity, and records a wealth of other information.

The monthly journal *Labour Market Trends* includes key statistical series from the *Labour Force Survey* (and other sources) by gender. It also publishes feature articles, including an annual article on women in the labour market. The *Labour Force Survey Quarterly Bulletin* covers Great Britain, while for Northern Ireland there is the *Northern Ireland Labour Force Survey Quarterly Report.* Information from the *Labour Force Survey* and other sources of labour force data (including detailed local information from the *Census of Population 1991* and administrative data) is held on *NOMIS*, a computer-based information system.

Unlike the *Labour Force Survey*, which collects information from individuals not in employment as well as those who are, surveys of employers cover only employees. For various reasons, low-paid and part-time workers are often under-represented in such surveys and this particularly affects the data on women. Employer surveys do, however, give an industrial breakdown which is consistent with economic data. Two examples are the *Annual Employment Survey* and the *New Earnings Survey* which cover Great Britain. A separate *Census of Employment* is carried out in Northern Ireland.

Separate Tables compares women's and men's employment and the *Briefings on Women and Men in Britain* series includes *The Labour Market* and *Work and Parenting*. *The Working Lives of Women and Men in Northern Ireland* provides similar data for Northern Ireland.

Several studies have considered issues related to combining work and parenting. The *Family and Working Lives Survey* collected retrospective data on life events and working patterns, while other surveys have collected information from the parents of babies and young children and their employers. Recent publications include *Mothers, Fathers and Employment, Maternity Rights and Benefits in Britain 1996* and *Family Friendly Working Arrangements in Britain 1996*.

5. Health and social care

A substantial amount of material is collected and published by gender on health and social care, either via administrative returns by health and local authorities or through government and other surveys, some of which are described below. Unfortunately, much of the data does not cover the United Kingdom as a whole.

A primary source of data on personal health status is the large-scale annual *Health Survey for England*. Additionally, *The Health of Adult Britain* combines census, survey and administrative data to show trends in health from 1841 onwards. The *General Household Survey* and *Continuous Household Survey* regularly contain data on smoking and drinking, health conditions and treatments, cross-tabulated with social factors and disaggregated by gender.

Gender information on the use of services is available from National Health Service and Department of Social Security administrative data and also from surveys. Examples of useful publications include *Hospital Episode Statistics, Health and Personal Social Services for England, Health and Personal Social Services Statistics (Northern Ireland), Health Statistics Wales* and *Scottish Health Statistics.* The *Survey of Psychiatric Morbidity in Great Britain* provides data on mental disorders and the provision of related care, the *Family Resources Survey* publishes information on carers and those needing care, and the publication *Health Inequalities* looks at patterns of inequality in health.

There are gender-disaggregated statistics available from the Department of Health on National Health Service staff, but none on social services staff at present, although there are plans to collect these data in the near future.

6. Income and housing

Although most of the data on income are collected for individuals, analyses are generally published for households, families or benefit units and therefore not by gender. The annual *Family Expenditure Survey* and *Family Resources Survey* collect detailed information on expenditure and income and some gender analyses are possible using the microdata at the Data Archive, even though these analyses are not currently included in the publications. Data from these surveys are also published in *Households Below Average Income*, which analyses income as an indication of living standards and shows changes over time, by gender.

Two of the topics in the *Briefings on Women and Men in Britain* series cover financial information: *Pay* and *Income and Personal Finance*. The latter contains analysis of individual income from the *Family Expenditure Survey*. In addition, levels of income from all sources, including pensions and savings, are shown in *Women and Men in Britain 1995 - The Life Cycle of Inequality*. Other studies have considered specific income issues. For example, *Lone Parents, Work and Benefits* gives the results of a study of lone parents and their material circumstances.

Earnings information by gender is available in *Labour Market Trends, New Earnings Survey* and *Labour Force Survey Quarterly Bulletin* and some data are included in *Separate Tables*. Social security data gathered from administrative sources are available by gender on a range of benefit and allowance claimants in *Social Security Statistics*.

Similar problems arise with housing statistics, which are mostly published in terms of household, not individual, characteristics. Information is sometimes presented according to the characteristics of the household reference person (previously termed the head of household), including whether that person is male or female. This is not a problem for one-person households, but the present definition makes the male partner the household reference person for nearly all couples. The definition is under review.

7. Crime and justice

A variety of administrative data is collected from the police, the courts, the probation service and prisons, covering crimes committed, prosecutions, convictions and sentences served. Again, however, consistent coverage of the United Kingdom is not always possible. Gender-disaggregated data are found in the annual publications *Criminal Statistics England and Wales*, *Criminal Proceedings in Scottish Courts*, *Prison Statistics England and Wales* and *A Commentary on Northern Ireland Crime Statistics*. The biennial *British Crime Survey* is the best source of information on the gender of victims of crime, and other household surveys (such as the *General Household Survey* and *Continuous Household Survey*) cover this topic from time to time.

8. Transport and environment

Published statistics on transport and environmental issues which are disaggregated by gender are limited. The *National Travel Survey* is used to estimate distances travelled and mode of travel, including the use of transport by disabled people, and international travel is covered by the *International Passenger Survey*. The *Census of Population* carries questions on vehicle ownership and detailed information on travel to work, while statistics on road accidents are published in *Road Accidents Great Britain*.

On wider environmental issues, the main published sources of gender statistics relating to the environment consist of surveys of public attitudes, such as the *Survey of Public Attitudes to the Environment* and the *British Social Attitudes Report*, which includes an occasional module on the environment. The Health and Safety Executive collects and publishes a range of work-related environmental health topics and gender analyses can be provided.

9. Lifestyles

Data are available on a variety of activities such as how people spend their time, which leisure activities they undertake, their viewing and reading habits, religion and holidays. Both the *General Household Survey* and the *British Social Attitudes Report* (*Continuous Household Survey* and *Northern Ireland Social Attitudes Survey* for Northern Ireland) collect a range of information on lifestyles and behaviour including trends over time. *Social Trends* has a regular chapter on lifestyles.

Published gender-disaggregated data on participation in the arts, sports or other cultural and community activities are patchy. Some are available from membership records of sports clubs, market research or surveys, and the *Digest of Sports Statistics for the United Kingdom 1990* uses a variety of sources to report on sports participation. *Cultural Trends* publishes statistics on various sectors of the arts, although the only figures published by gender are on book borrowing and television and cinema viewing. The National Readership Survey of newspaper- and magazine-reading habits has published data by gender in *Social Trends*.

The *International Passenger Survey* is the main source of statistics on international travel and tourism, and these can be analysed by age, length of stay, spending, purpose of visit and destination as well as gender. Information is collected on domestic tourism and is available from the Department of Culture, Media and Sport, although it is not published by gender.

One of the best indicators of lifestyle is actually to ask people how they spend their time, using a *Time Use Survey* in which respondents complete diaries of their day. No large-scale official *Time Use Survey* has yet been carried out in the United Kingdom, though a small-scale diary exercise was carried out as part of the Omnibus Survey in 1995. It is hoped to develop and fund a major survey in the near future as this would provide a data source able to cover a number of gender-related issues, including informal or unpaid activities, on which there is currently limited information.

Gender-related statistics by theme

Section 2: Alphabetical list of sources, publications and databases

Alphabetical list of sources, publications and databases

This section contains an alphabetical list of the sources mentioned in Section 1, together with bibliographical information, more detail on the content of the source, so far as it relates to gender statistics, and a list of the relevant keywords which are cross-referenced in the index. Where data from a particular source are published in more than one place, the latest major publication is listed. In most cases, a list of other publications is available from the appropriate contact in Section 3.

1 ▷ Annual Employment Survey

ISBN: 1 85774 245 1
Publisher: Office for National Statistics
Price: £25 per part (in two parts)
Frequency: Annual
Author: Office for National Statistics

The *Annual Employment Survey* is a sample survey of 125,000 enterprises and is the main source of information for the numbers of people employed in local areas, by detailed industrial categories, throughout Great Britain. The statistics are all provided in gender-disaggregated format, cross-referenced by full and part-time status, and are the only employment data available at such a level, covering all sections of the economy.

Keywords: Employer size; Employment; Employment patterns; Hours worked; Industry of employment; Sector of employment.

Briefings on Women and Men in Britain

Pay, The Labour Market, Education and Vocational Training in England and Wales, Education and Vocational Training in Scotland, Management and the Professions, Work and Parenting, Income and Personal Finance
Publisher: Equal Opportunities Commission
Price: Free publications
Frequency: *Ad-hoc* (1997)
Author: Equal Opportunities Commission
This set of seven *Briefings* covers a range of areas relating to the positions of women and men in Britain. Each *Briefing* comprises one page of policy points and three pages of graphics and commentary. Where possible the briefings take a 20 year perspective, looking at changes over the lifetime of the Sex Discrimination and Equal Pay Acts.
Keywords: Benefits received; Dependent children; Education; Employment; Family; Income; Occupation; Pay; Pensions; Vocational training.

British Adult Literacy Survey

Published in *Adult Literacy in Britain 1997*
ISBN: 0 11 620943 7
Publisher: The Stationery Office
Price: £30
Frequency: *Ad-hoc* (1997)
Author: Siobhán Carey, Sampson Low and Jacqui Hansbro
This survey was conducted as part of an international programme of surveys known as the International Adult Literacy Survey. It interviewed 3,811 adults living in private households. Literacy is determined as a broad range of skills required in a varied range of contexts, implying that literacy goes beyond merely reading or comprehending text to include a broader range of skills in using information in texts. Gender disaggregation is published on the topics referenced by the keywords below.
Keywords: Economic activity; Employment patterns; Literacy; Occupation; Qualifications obtained.

4 British Cohort Study 1970

Published in *Twenty-something in the 1990s*
ISBN: 1 840 14 014 3
Publisher: Ashgate Publishing
Price: £30
Frequency: *Ad hoc* (1997)
Author: Social Statistics Research Unit, City University
The 1970 British Cohort Study, originally the British Births Survey, includes everybody born in one week in 1970 (17,198 individuals). The aim is to record medical, physical, educational and social development, and to study their influence on the life-cycle. Data were collected at birth, and from four follow-ups at ages five, 10, 16 and 26; *Twenty-something in the 1990s* reports on the 1996 survey. The datasets are deposited with the Data Archive and a full list of publications is available from the Social Statistics Research Unit at City University.
Keywords: Attitudes; Children; Crimes committed; Education; Employment; Health; Literacy; Longitudinal analysis; Marital status; Qualifications obtained; Social group.

5 British Crime Survey

Publisher: Home Office
Price: Free
Frequency: Every two years
Author: Home Office
The British Crime Survey (BCS) is a sample survey of approximately 15,000 adults in England and Wales. It covers people's experience of crime, their perceptions of crime and their contacts with the police. The last few surveys have also covered self-reported illegal drug taking, and special reports have been published on topics such as sexual victimisation.
Keywords: Attitudes; Crime; Drug use; Experience of crime; Victims of crime.

British Household Panel Survey　6

Published in *Changing Households: The British Household Panel Survey 1990-1992*
ISBN:　1 85871 102 9
Publisher:　ESRC Research Centre on Micro-Social Change in Britain
Price:　£14.50
Frequency: *Ad hoc* (1994)
Author:　Nick Buck, Jonathan Gershuny, David Rose and Jacqueline Scott
This survey is a longitudinal survey of the members of a random sample of households, which attempts to improve the understanding of processes, causes and effects of social change. The original sample size was 10,262 adults. *Changing Households* includes results from the first three waves of the survey. It contains articles on several gender-related topics, including changes in household and family composition, and changes in economic activity and work. There are now six waves of the *British Household Panel Survey* available for analysis via the Data Archive and working papers on the survey are available from the ESRC Research Centre on Micro-Social Change in Britain at Essex University.
Keywords: Attitudes; Debt; Earnings; Economic activity; Employment; Employment histories; Health; Household and family composition; Housing; Income; Longitudinal analysis; Savings.

British Social Attitudes Report　7

ISBN:　1 85521 607 8
Publisher: Dartmouth Publishing Company
Price:　£25
Frequency: Annual (sometimes published as *International Social Attitudes*)
Author:　Social and Community Planning Research
The *British Social Attitudes Survey* of around 3,000 individuals is carried out and published annually and seeks to chart changes in British social values during the 1980s and 1990s in relation to other changes in society. Different topics are covered each year, and articles on gender roles and differing attitudes of women and men are often included. For example, the 12th report from 1995/96 includes a chapter on the factors influencing whether mothers work. The dataset is available through the Data Archive so that further analyses can be carried out.
Keywords: Attitudes; Childcare; Crime; Employment; Environment; Family composition; Leisure; Religion.

Section 2

8 Census of Employment (Northern Ireland)

Publisher: Northern Ireland Department of Economic Development
Price: Free
Frequency: Every two years
Author: Northern Ireland Department of Economic Development
This statutory census has been carried out in Northern Ireland every two years since 1987. It is a full count of employees in all industries except the self-employed and those in agriculture.
Keywords: Employment; Industry of employment; Number of employees.

9 Census of Population 1991

The *Census of Population* takes place every 10 years and is an authoritative account of people and housing in Britain. Comparable statistics are produced for very fine geographical areas and the data also allow the cross-classification of various population and housing characteristics. The outputs from the Census are made available in printed reports of summary statistics for geographical areas or particular topics and also as tailor-made statistical abstracts for smaller areas or populations. Samples of Anonymised Records are also available for further research and analysis. A list of outputs is available from Census Marketing in the Office for National Statistics.
Keywords: Car ownership; Country of birth; Demographic characteristics; Economic activity; Ethnic group; Gaelic language; Household composition; Housing; Long-term illness; Migration; Property characteristics; Qualifications obtained; Social group; Tenure arrangements; Travel to work; Welsh language.

A Commentary on Northern Ireland Crime Statistics   10

ISBN: 0 337 03092 8
Publisher: The Stationery Office
Price: £8.75
Frequency: Annual
Author: Northern Ireland Office
This publication reports on administrative information on criminal offences in Northern Ireland with some presented by gender.
Keywords: Court cases; Crimes and offences committed; Prison population.

Continuous Household Survey (Northern Ireland)   11

Publisher: Northern Ireland Statistics and Research Agency
Price: Free
Frequency: Under review, but last published in 1994 covering 1991-93 data.
Author: Northern Ireland Statistics and Research Agency
This is a a multi-purpose survey based on a sample of 4,500 private households in Northern Ireland; it has been running since 1983. The nature and aims of the *Continuous Household Survey* are similar to those of the *General Household Survey*. Data are collected on five core topics: education, employment, health, housing, and population and family information, with other topics covered periodically. The data are available for further analysis at the Data Archive.
Keywords: Care provided; Care received; Childcare; Experience of crime; GP consultations; Health; Household composition; Household income; Leisure; Long-term illness; Occupation; Qualifications obtained; Social class.

12 ▸ Control of Immigration: Statistics United Kingdom

ISBN: 0 10 137372 4
Publisher: The Stationery Office
Price: £19
Frequency: Annual
Author: Home Office
This publication contains information on entry to, and settlement in, the United Kingdom. The statistics are generally available by gender.
Keywords: Asylum; Immigration.

13 ▸ Criminal Statistics England and Wales

ISBN: 0 10 120102 2
Publisher: The Stationery Office
Price: £22.70
Frequency: Annual
Author: Home Office
Annual data are published in a report which contains statistics drawn from administrative information on criminal offences. Most statistics are given by gender.
Keywords: Court cases; Crimes and offences committed; Criminal careers/histories; Offenders.

14 ▸ Criminal Proceedings in Scottish Courts

ISBN: 0 7480 6213 0
Publisher: Scottish Office
Price: £2
Frequency: Annual
Author: Scottish Office Home Department
This bulletin contains information on the types of crime or offence involved in court proceedings and on the gender and age of offenders as centrally recorded by the police.
Keywords: Court cases; Crime.

Cultural Trends

15

Publisher: Policy Studies Institute
Price: £68 per annum (£17.95 per issue)
Frequency: Quarterly
Author: Policy Studies Institute
This is a quarterly publication which brings together an extensive range of information on the cultural sector and some audience figures are disaggregated by gender.
Keywords: Arts; Employment; Leisure; Tourism; Visitors.

Digest of Sports Statistics for the United Kingdom 1990

16

ISBN: 1 872158 25 0
Publisher: Ancient House Press, Ipswich
Price: Free
Frequency: *Ad hoc* (1991)
Author: Sports Council
This occasional digest draws on a wide variety of data sources to compile individual profiles of sports or categories of sport. The sources include membership records, market research, the Great Britain *General Household Survey* and the Northern Ireland *Continuous Household Survey*. Each section has a membership profile which gives any available data for the gender of participants. The latest data available refer to 1990.
Keywords: Leisure; Sports participation.

17 Education Statistics for the United Kingdom

ISBN: 0 11 270992 3
Publisher: The Stationery Office
Price: £15
Frequency: Annual
Author: Department for Education and Employment

This annual publication is the primary source of education statistics for the United Kingdom as a whole. The majority of the statistics, taken from administrative records, are broken down by gender and the latest report available is for 1996. For 1997, this publication will be combined with *Training Statistics* to produce a new publication *Education and Training Statistics in the United Kingdom.*

Keywords: Absence from schools; Education; Examination results; Qualifications obtained; School leavers; Schools; Students; Teaching and academic staff.

18 Equality Now and Then

Publisher: Equal Opportunities Commission for Northern Ireland
Price: Free
Frequency: Annual
Author: Equal Opportunities Commission for Northern Ireland

A brief report giving a picture of the changes over time in women's and men's experience of employment, pay, public life and education.

Keywords: Earnings; Economic activity; Education; Employment; Industry of employment; Occupation; Public life.

Ethnic Minorities in Britain: Diversity and Disadvantage

19

ISBN: 0 85374 670 2
Publisher: Policy Studies Institute
Price: £17.50
Frequency: *Ad hoc* (1997)
Author: T Modood, R Berthoud et al

This study surveyed 8,000 individuals in England and Wales, of whom 5,200 were from ethnic minorities. It is the fourth in a series of major studies which charts the experiences of ethnic minorities in Britain since the 1960s and reports on changes in such key fields as family and household structures, education, qualifications and employment. Although the published data are not always disaggregated by gender, anonymised records are available at the Data Archive for further analysis.

Keywords: Economic activity; Employment; Ethnic group; Examination results; Family composition; Health; Housing; Income.

Ethnic Minority Women and the Labour Market: Analysis of the 1991 Census

20

ISBN: 1 807358 24 4
Publisher: Equal Opportunities Commission
Price: £14.95
Frequency: *Ad hoc* (1994)
Author: David Owen, Centre for Research in Ethnic Relations, University of Warwick

This report provides information on the geographical patterns of variations in the labour market situation for women from different ethnic groups. Comparisons are made with men, and with women from different ethnic groups. There is an accompanying volume of tables.

Keywords: Education; Employment; Government training; Labour market; Population; Unemployment.

21 Facts About Women and Men Series

Facts about Women and Men in Great Britain
Facts about Women and Men in Scotland
Facts about Women and Men in Wales/Ffeithiau am Fenywod a Dynion yng Nghymru

Publisher: Equal Opportunities Commission
Price: Free
Frequency: Annual
Author: Equal Opportunities Commission

An annual series of statistics cards, each containing a selection of tables chosen to provide a picture of the relative position of women and men. The 1997 editions also contain a selection of Equality Indicators.

Keywords: Dependent children; Earnings; Economic activity; Employment; Ethnic origin; Examination results; Hours worked; Industry of employment; Marital status; Occupation; Population; Students.

22 Family and Working Lives Survey

Published as *Family and Working Lives Data Source Book, 1997 (Volumes 1-3)*
Publisher: Department for Education and Employment
Price: Free
Frequency: *Ad hoc* (1997)
Author: Department for Education and Employment

This retrospective life history survey of adults aged 16-69 is an update of the *Women in Employment Survey*, which dates back to 1980 and looked at elements of women's lives affecting employment. The *Family and Working Lives Survey* includes male respondents and allows a direct comparison between the work of men and women to see how these may be changing. The sample size was of 11,237 adults. The data are deposited at the Data Archive.

Keywords: Benefits received; Disability; Education; Employment; Family; Housing; Longitudinal analysis; Pensions; Trade Union membership; Training; Unemployment.

Family Expenditure Survey - see *Family Spending*

Family Friendly Working Arrangements in Britain 1996   23

ISBN: 0 85522 615 3
Publisher: Department for Education and Employment
Price: £4.95
Frequency: *Ad hoc* (1997)
Author: John Forth, Steve Lissenburgh, Claire Callender and Neil Millward
This report presents research findings on family friendly working arrangments, and is based on three nationally representative, large-scale surveys of mothers, fathers and employers carried out in spring 1996 by the Policy Studies Institute on behalf of the Department for Education and Employment, DTI and Department of Social Security. It is published as *Department for Education and Employment Research Report RR16*.
Keywords: Benefits received; Employment; Employment patterns; Maternity rights; Paternity leave; Pay.

Family Resources Survey   24

ISBN: 0 11 762537 X
Publisher: The Stationery Office
Price: £28
Frequency: Annual
Author: Department of Social Security
The *Family Resources Survey* covers Great Britain and has been carried out annually since 1993-94. It collects information on the living standards and circumstances of 26,000 private households in Great Britain, but because most of the published data are at the household level, gender disaggregation does not feature widely in the report. However, the report does publish information by gender on carers and those needing care. A wide range of analyses (see keywords below) are possible from the micro-data which are available from the Data Archive. The most recent published data available are for 1995-96.
Keywords: Benefits received; Care provided; Care received; Household assets; Household income; Pay; Social class; Unemployment.

25 Family Spending

ISBN: 0 11 620947 X
Publisher: The Stationery Office
Price: £37.50
Frequency: Annual
Author: Office for National Statistics

The *Family Expenditure Survey* has been in existence since 1957 and is a sample with responses from around 6,500 private households in the United Kingdom which provides information on household expenditure and income. Because most of the published data are at the household level, gender disaggregation does not feature widely in the report, but analyses (see keywords below) are possible from the micro-data, which are available from the Data Archive. The most recent published data available are for 1996-97.

Keywords: Household composition; Household expenditure; Household income; Social class.

General Household Survey - see *Living in Britain*

26 Getting Around After 60

ISBN: 0 11 321966 0
Publisher: The Stationery Office
Price: £19.95
Frequency: *Ad hoc* (1996)
Author: C Jarvis, R Hancock, J Askham, A Tinker

This publication about the activities and characteristics of the over 60s contains gender disaggregated analyses on a cross-section of topics from a wide range of data sources, including major government surveys.

Keywords: Care provided; Care received; Disability; Employment; Housing; Income.

Health and Personal Social Services Statistics for England · 27

ISBN: 11 3 220 138
Publisher: The Stationery Office
Price: £75
Frequency: Annual
Author: Department of Health
This is an annual compendium of data collected mainly from administrative returns made by health authorities, local authorities, National Health Service Trusts and other authorities, giving an overall view of many aspects of health in England. Gender data are available on the keywords given.
Keywords: Admissions to hospital; Cancer registrations; Death rates; Drinking patterns; Health; Health service staff; Home help; Life expectancy; Smoking trends.

Health and Personal Social Services Statistics (Northern Ireland) · 28

Publisher: Department of Health and Social Security (Northern Ireland)
Price: Free
Frequency: Occasional
Author: Department of Health and Social Security (Northern Ireland)
This contains similar information to the publication for England (see above).
Keywords: Admissions to hospital; Cancer registrations; Death rates; Diseases; Health; Home help.

29 Health Inequalities

ISBN: 0 11 620942 9
Publisher: The Stationery Office
Price: £35
Frequency: Every 10 years
Author: Office for National Statistics

This decennial publication presents analysis of the current patterns of health inequalities in order to assess if they are getting better or worse. It therefore contains a wide selection of health data from a variety of sources cross-classified with social factors, much of which is presented in gender-disaggregated form. The latest report was published in 1997.

Keywords: Death rates; Health; Life expectancy; Long-term illness; Population.

30 The Health of Adult Britain

ISBN: VOL 1 - 0 11 691695 8
VOL 2 - 0 11 691696 6
Publisher: The Stationery Office
Price: £60 (2 volumes)
Frequency: *Ad hoc* (1997)
Author: Office for National Statistics

This publication covers trends in illness and death in Britain from 1841 to 1994. The information is drawn from administrative data and health surveys.

Keywords: Death rates; Dietary behaviour; Health; Illness; Smoking trends.

Health Statistics Wales

ISBN: 0 7504 1526 6
Publisher: Welsh Office
Price: £7
Frequency: Annual
Author: Welsh Office
This publication contains summary text, along with graphics and tables that illustrate the range of healthcare services in Wales. Gender data are available on the topics covered by the keywords.
Keywords: Cancer registrations; Cause of death; Consultant episodes; GP consultations; Health; Health service staff; Smoking trends.

Health Survey for England

ISBN: 0 11 322 0219
Publisher: The Stationery Office
Price: £60
Frequency: Annual
Author: Department of Health
This is a continuous household survey which collects data from around 17,000 adults and children over 2 in England. The survey itself consists of health and socio-economic questionnaires, physical measurement and a blood sample, and all the data in the survey are published by gender. The latest results are for 1995, published during 1997.
Keywords: Accidents; Dietary behaviour; Drinking patterns; Health; Long-term illness; Smoking trends.

33 Hospital Episode Statistics

ISBN: 1 85839 624 7; 1 85839 627 1; 1 85839 628 X
Publisher: The Stationery Office
Price: £75 (three volume set)
Frequency: Annual
Author: Department of Health

This three-volume publication covering England contains details of completed hospital episodes (periods of patient care under one consultant within one healthcare provider) analysed by diagnosis and by operative procedure. These data enable the National Health Service, and medical and other researchers, to analyse trends in morbidity and patterns of treatment, and to monitor and investigate the reasons for variations between regions and between Health Authority Districts.

Keywords: Admissions to hospital; Consultant episodes; Diagnoses; Discharge from hospital; Health.

34 Households Below Average Income: A Statistical Analysis 1979-1994/95

ISBN: 0 11 762552 3
Publisher: The Stationery Office
Price: £33
Frequency: Annual
Author: Department of Social Security

This report is an analysis of incomes as an indicator of the living standards that individuals can attain. It provides estimates of patterns of personal disposable income in the United Kingdom and of the changes over time, concentrating on the lower part of the income distribution, but providing comparisons with the upper part where appropriate. The analyses are based primarily on the *Family Expenditure Survey* and to a lesser extent on the *Family Resources Survey*. Topics covered include the income distribution of various sections of society and a comment on the broad changes that have occurred since 1979. There is a longitudinal component that traces the income experience of particular individuals and provides an examination of expenditure changes since 1979.

Keywords: Economic activity; Family composition; Household income; Longitudinal analysis.

International Passenger Survey - see *Travel Trends*

Labour Force Survey - see *Labour Force Survey Quarterly Bulletin*
and *Northern Ireland Labour Force Survey Quarterly Report*

Labour Force Survey Quarterly Bulletin

35

ISSN: 0967 5876
Publisher: Office for National Statistics
Price: £30 per annum
Frequency: Quarterly
Author: Office for National Statistics

This quarterly bulletin presents comprehensive results from the Labour Force
Survey, which is a quarterly survey of 60,000 households made up of five waves of
approximately 12,000. It covers topics on the labour market such as employment
and unemployment. For gender-disaggregated data, see list of keywords. (The
Quarterly Bulletin is likely to be replaced by a new Labour Force Survey
Supplement to *Labour Market Trends* during 1998.)

Keywords: Earnings; Economic activity; Employment; Employment patterns;
Ethnic group; Hours worked; Industry of employment; Job-related training;
Labour market; Longitudinal analysis; Occupation; Unemployment.

36 Labour Market Trends (incorporating Employment Gazette)

ISSN: 1361-4819
Publisher: The Stationery Office
Price: £6 (£63.50 per annum)
Frequency: Monthly
Author: Office for National Statistics

This monthly journal contains a wide range of gender-disaggregated information on the labour market, including area statistics. It also carries articles, including some specific to particular groups in the labour market such as part-timers, women, ethnic groups and older workers, with an index to this information published annually.

Keywords: Earnings; Economic activity; Employment; Employment pattern; Hours worked; Industry of employment; Job-related training; Labour market; Occupation; Unemployment;

37 Living in Britain

ISBN: 0 11 691550 1
Publisher: The Stationery Office
Price: £30
Frequency: Annual
Author: Office for National Statistics

This report provides gender-disaggregated information on the socio-demographic topics covered by the *General Household Survey*. The *General Household Survey* is a multi-purpose continuous sample survey of approximately 9,000 households and about 20,000 adults aged 16 and over in Great Britian. Data are collected on five core topics: education, employment, health, housing, and population and family information with other topics covered periodically. Reports for each year generally cover the extra topics covered by that year's survey and a list of these can be found in each report. The core data are published in *Living In Britain* with most analyses disaggregated by gender. The micro-data are available at the Data Archive. The 1997 report published the results of the 1995-96 survey. The survey was suspended for 1997-98 but resumed the following year.

Keywords: Care provided; Care received; Childcare; Ethnic group; Experience of crime; GP consultations; Health; Household composition; Household income; Leisure; Long-term illness; Occupation; Qualifications obtained; Social class.

Lone Parents, Work and Benefits 38

ISBN: 0 11 762450 0
Publisher: The Stationery Office
Price: £25
Frequency: *Ad hoc* (1997)
Author: Alan Marsh, Reuben Ford and Louise Finlayson
This fourth report from the Department of Social Security/Policy Studies Institute Programme of Research into Low Income Families (PRILIF) presents results from a nationally representative survey of 880 lone parents in Britain, which was carried out in 1994. The two main purposes of the survey were: to monitor lone parents' family circumstances, material welfare and labour market participation; and to evaluate the impact of the introduction of the Child Support Agency in April 1993. It was published as *Department of Social Security Research Report no. 61*.
Keywords: Benefits received; Employment; Family composition; Income.

Longitudinal Study 39

Published in *Longitudinal Study 1971-1991: History, Organisation and Quality of Data*
ISBN: 0 11 691637 0
Publisher: The Stationery Office
Price: £27.30
Frequency: *Ad hoc* (1995)
Author: L Hattersley & R Creeser
This study is a 1% sample of the population of England and Wales containing linked census and vital events data. It was originally drawn from the resident population enumerated at the 1971 Census and based on four dates of birth. The study now contains linked records from the 1971 Census, 1981 Census, 1991 Census and events registration as they occurred for each member in the study. The sample size from the 1991 Census was 543,884. Broad subject areas include all census information and geography, occupational mortality, fertility, cancer, migration, household data and families. Micro-data are accessible via the Office for National Statistics and the Social Statistics Research Unit at City University. A full publication list is available from the Social Statistics Research Unit, City University.
Keywords: Cancer survival; Country of birth; Family composition; Fertility rates; Housing; Longitudinal analysis; Long-term illness; Migration; Property characteristics; Qualifications obtained; Tenure arrangements.

40 Maternity Rights and Benefits in Britain 1996

ISBN: 0 11 762536 1
Publisher: The Stationery Office
Price: £35
Frequency: *Ad hoc* (1997)
Author: Claire Callender, Neil Millward, Steve Lissenburgh and John Forth
This report presents research findings on the impact of changes to the legislation on maternity rights and benefits, and is based on two nationally representative, large-scale surveys carried out in spring 1996 by the Policy Studies Institute on behalf of the Department for Education and Employment, DTI and Department of Social Security. Similar surveys were carried out by Policy Studies Institute in 1979 and 1988/89. Published as *Department of Social Security Research Report no. 67*.
Keywords: Benefits received; Employment; Maternity rights; Paternity leave; Pay.

41 Mothers, Fathers and Employment

ISBN: 0 85522 595 5
Publisher: Department for Education and Employment, *Research Report 10*
Price: £4.95
Frequency: *Ad hoc* (1997)
Author: Julia Brannen, Peter Moss, Charlie Owen and Chris Whale
This report draws on secondary analysis of the *Labour Force Survey* to analyse the employment position of mothers and fathers with dependent children over the period from 1984 to 1994.
Keywords: Dependent children; Employment; Employment patterns; Hours worked.

MRC National Survey of Health and Development — 42

published in *The Imprint of Time*
ISBN: 0 19 827360 6
Publisher: Oxford University Press
Price: £30
Frequency: *Ad hoc* (1991)
Author: M E J Wadsworth
This is a longitudinal sample survey of all single, legitimate births in England, Scotland and Wales in one week in 1946 (5,362 individuals). The initial aim of informing planning of obstetric care in the emerging National Health Service was subsequently widened to study experiences and events, and their relationship to changes in health and ageing. This report describes the study's findings up to 1989. A full publication list is available from University College London Medical School, Department of Epidemiology and Public Health.
Keywords: Children; Education; Employment; Family; Health; Longitudinal analysis; Occupation.

National Child Development Study — 43

Published in *Life at 33: The fifth follow-up of the National Child Development Study*
ISBN: 1 874579 11 3
Publisher: National Children's Bureau
Price: £13.50
Frequency: *Ad hoc* (1993)
Author: National Children's Bureau
The *National Child Development Study* is a longitudinal survey of an initial sample of 17,000 people born in 1958, and has so far followed them from birth with follow-up at the ages of 7, 11, 16, 23 and 33. The aim is to study physical and mental development and changes in social and economic status. *Life at 33* reports the first findings of the fifth follow-up of the study, and provides a picture linking earlier circumstances, experiences and characteristics with the situation at 33. A working paper series is produced by the Social Statistics Research Unit, City University.
Keywords: Attitudes; Children; Education; Employment; Employment histories; Family; Health; Housing; Income; Longitudinal analysis; Qualifications obtained; Social group; Training.

44 ▷ National Travel Survey

ISBN: 0 11 551976 9
Publisher: The Stationery Office
Price: £20
Frequency: Annual
Author: Department of the Environment, Transport and the Regions
This survey began in 1988, following *ad hoc* surveys from 1965 to 1985/86. It is a continuous survey covering approximately 5,040 households each year, and all household members are interviewed and complete a travel diary for one week. The data are published annually and cover three years' combined data. This survey is carried out in order to provide a better understanding of the use of transport facilities made by different sectors of the community, and much of the analysis is by gender.
Keywords: Car ownership; Distance travelled; Journeys; Transport; Travel.

45 ▷ New Earnings Survey

ISBN: 0 11 620935 6
Publisher: The Stationery Office
Price: £22 per volume (£110 for all six volumes)
Frequency: Annual
Author: Office for National Statistics
This annual sample survey has been held in broadly the same form since 1970. The main purpose of the survey is to obtain information about the levels, distribution and make-up of earnings of employees in all industries and occupations and about the collective agreements which cover them. The survey is based each year on a 1% sample of employees who are members of Pay-As-You-Earn income tax schemes. The sample of over 200,000 each year comprises all those whose national insurance numbers end with a specified pair of digits. Low-paid workers are under-represented in the *New Earnings Survey*, because of its use of Pay As You Earn tax records and this affects women disproportionately. A project is currently under way to rectify this. The data are published by gender in six volumes.
Keywords: Hours worked; Industry of employment; Occupation; Pay; Pensions; Sector of employment.

NOMIS (National Online Manpower Information Service)

Publisher: Office for National Statistics
Price: Subscription charges plus on-line time charges vary by type of user.
NOMIS is an on-line labour market information system run for the Office for National Statistics by the University of Durham. The system contains more than 70 data sets covering all official sources down to the lowest available geographical disaggregation. The data can often be disaggregated by gender.
Keywords: Benefits received; Earnings; Economic activity; Employment; Employment patterns; Job-related training; Labour market; Unemployment.

Northern Ireland Labour Force Survey Quarterly Report

Publisher: Northern Ireland Department of Economic Development
Price: Free
Frequency: Quarterly
Author: Northern Ireland Department of Economic Development
This quarterly report presents comprehensive results from the *Labour Force Survey of Northern Ireland*, which is a quarterly survey of around 3,250 addresses in five waves of around 650 private households. For gender-disaggregated data, see list of keywords.
Keywords: Earnings; Economic activity; Employment; Employment patterns; Hours worked; Job-related training; Labour market; Longitudinal analysis; Occupation; Unemployment.

48 Northern Ireland Social Attitudes Survey

ISBN: 0 86281 637 8
Publisher: Appletree Press, Belfast
Price: £20
Frequency: Annual
Author: Lizanne Dowds, Paula Devine and Richard Breen

The *Northern Ireland Social Attitudes Survey* of around 900 adults is the sister survey of the *British Social Attitudes Survey* and provides a measure of the development of social attitudes. Some core modules are included every year, with others included as appropriate.

Keywords: Attitudes; Childcare; Employment; Environment; Experience of crime; Family composition; Leisure; Religion.

49 Population Trends

ISSN: 0307 4463
Publisher: The Stationery Office
Price: £16.50 (£60 per annum)
Frequency: Quarterly
Author: Office for National Statistics

This brings together a wide variety of data into a regular series of tables and articles on subjects such as births, deaths and migration. All the data are disaggregated by gender where appropriate.

Keywords: Birth rates; Death rates; Emigration; Life expectancy; Migration; Population; Population estimates; Population projections.

Prison Statistics England and Wales

ISBN: 0 10 137322 8
Publisher: The Stationery Office
Price: £18.30
Frequency: Annual
Author: Home Office
Administrative data on persons held in custody are published annually and disaggregated by gender where appropriate. As well as disaggregated statistics on the prison population, receptions and discharges, cross-referenced with other factors such as offence, the report gives detailed breakdowns (including by gender) of different prison populations: for example, remand prisoners, sentenced prisoners, young offenders and ethnic origin.
Keywords: Crime; Criminal career/histories; Offenders; Prison population.

Regional Trends

ISBN: 0 11 620837 6
Publisher: The Stationery Office
Price: £37.50
Frequency: Annual
Author: Office for National Statistics
Regional Trends is an annual compendium publication containing the most comprehensive official statistics about the regions of the United Kingdom. It also contains key data for the sub-regions and local authority districts. Some of the data are published in gender-disaggregated form, and for the topics which are best covered see keywords below.
Keywords: Court cases; Death rates; Earnings; Economic activity; Employment patterns; Examination results; Industry of employment; Population estimates; Unemployment.

52 Road Accidents Great Britain

ISBN: 0 11 551972 6
Publisher: The Stationery Office
Price: £15
Frequency: Annual
Author: Department of the Environment, Transport and the Regions

The *Road Accidents Great Britain* report is an annual publication which gives statistics of road accidents and their resulting casualties. Most of the data are obtained from injury accident reports (collected by local police forces), from death registrations and coroners' and procurators' fiscal reports, as well as from traffic and vehicle registration data. The numbers of deaths and casualties are available by gender.

Keywords: Accidents; Casualties due to road accidents; Deaths from road accidents.

53 Scottish Health Statistics

ISSN: 0559 1953
Publisher: National Health Service (Scotland)
Price: £15
Frequency: Annual
Author: National Health Service (Scotland)

This is the main compendium of data from the National Health Service in Scotland and on many aspects of health in Scotland. For information which is gender-disaggregated see keywords, but other patient information can be disaggregated on request.

Keywords: Admissions to hospital; Cancer registrations; Death rates; Diagnoses; Diseases; Drug addicts; Health; Life expectancy; Smoking trends.

The Scottish School Leavers' Survey - Scotland's Young People: 19 in 1995

54

Publisher: The Scottish Office Education and Industry Department
Price: £37.50
Frequency: *Ad hoc* (1995)
Author: S Taylor

The equivalent in Scotland of the *Youth Cohort Study*, the *Scottish School Leavers' Survey* has undergone several re-designs in the short period it has been in existence. This report presents analyses from the fourth survey, which consisted of questionnaires at 16/17 and 18/19 of approximately 6,000 school leavers. The fifth survey will use a new design, consisting of three questionnaires at ages 16/17, 18/19 and 22/23.

Keywords: Attitudes; Employment; Family; Longitudinal analysis; Qualifications obtained; School leavers; Schools; Training.

Separate Tables

55

ISBN: 0 8 5522 550 5
Publisher: Department for Education and Employment
Price: Free
Frequency: *Ad hoc* (1997)
Author: Department for Education and Employment

This compares the achievements of men and women in education, training and employment. The data are drawn from regular statistical series and published reports and as a result vary in geographical coverage and time-periods.

Keywords: Earnings; Education; Job-related training; Labour market; Lifetime learning; Qualifications obtained; Skills; Students; Teaching and academic staff.

Social Focus Series

This is a series of publications which paints a picture of different groups of people in contemporary society, drawing together statistical information from a wide variety of sources across the United Kingdom. Comprehensive further references and contacts for further information are provided for those who wish to explore the subject more deeply. The data are disaggregated by gender where appropriate.

56 Social Focus on Children

ISBN: 0 11 620655 1
Publisher: The Stationery Office
Price: £25
Frequency: *Ad hoc* (1994)
Author: Office for National Statistics
Keywords: Accidents; Children; Death rates; Disability; Drinking patterns; GP consultations; Offences; Population; Smoking trends; Sports participation; Victims of crime.

57 Social Focus on Ethnic Minorities

ISBN: 0 11 620793 0
Publisher: The Stationery Office
Price: £25
Frequency: *Ad hoc* (1996)
Author: Office for National Statistics
Keywords: Care provided; Drinking patterns; Economic activity; Ethnic group; GP consultations; Industry of employment; Job-related training; Smoking trends; Sports participation.

Social Focus on Families

ISBN: 0 11 620919 4
Publisher: The Stationery Office
Price: £30
Frequency: *Ad hoc* (1997)
Author: Office for National Statistics
Keywords: Care provided; Family; Hours worked; Household composition; Marital status; Offenders; Tenure arrangements, Time use.

Social Focus on Women

ISBN: 0 11 620713 2
Publisher: The Stationery Office
Price: £25
Frequency: *Ad hoc* (1995)
Author: Office for National Statistics
Keywords: Care provided; Cause of death; Economic activity; Income; Life expectancy; Marital status; Offences; Population; Smoking trends; Sports participation; Unemployment; Victims of crime.

Social Security Statistics

ISBN: 0 11 762535 3
Publisher: The Stationery Office
Price: £36
Frequency: Annual
Author: Department of Social Security
This report covers Great Britain and contains analysis of benefits claimants and recipients, mainly from Department of Social Security administrative sources. Most chapters contain an analysis by gender.
Keywords: Benefits received; Contributions made; Pensions; Unemployment.

61 ▷ Social Trends

ISBN: 0 11 620987 9
Publisher: The Stationery Office
Price: £39.50
Frequency: Annual
Author: Office for National Statistics

Social Trends is a major annual publication which draws together statistics from a wide range of government departments and other organisations to paint a broad picture of British society today and how it has been changing. Each chapter focuses on a different social policy area such as population, education and crime, and the information is often available by gender. The latest edition is *Social Trends 28,* published in 1998. For topics which best cover gender issues, see keywords below.

Keywords: Attitudes; Death rates; Education; Employment; Examination results; Family composition; Health; Household composition; Housing; Leisure; Life expectancy; Literacy; Marital status; Occupation; Offenders; Population estimates; Time use.

62 ▷ Survey of Psychiatric Morbidity in Great Britain

ISBN: 0 11 691627 3; 0 11 691653 2; 0 11 691669 9 (plus five others in series)
Publisher: The Stationery Office
Price: Various (series of eight reports)
Frequency: *Ad hoc* (1995 and 1996)
Author: Office for National Statistics

This survey comprises four studies carried out in 1993 and 1994. A survey of 10,000 adults in private households provides information on prevalence rates of defined, specific mental disorders, associated physical and social impairment and the provision of relevant health and social care. The published reports also give information on the other three psychiatric morbidity studies of residents in institutions, homeless people and those with psychotic illnesses. All the data are presented by gender and the micro-data are held at the Data Archive.

Keywords: Health; Illness; Psychiatric illness.

1993 Survey of Public Attitudes to the Environment

Publisher: Department of the Environment, Transport and the Regions
Price: £5
Frequency: *Ad hoc* (1994)
Author: Department of the Environment, Transport and the Regions
This survey investigates public concern about the environment by gender, social class and area. Questions on attitudes to the environment cover strength of feeling, perceptions of government action and other attitudes. The data are mostly published in gender-disaggregated format.
Keywords: Attitudes; Environment.

Time Use Survey

A full Time Use Survey has not yet been carried out in the United Kingdom, but simple time use data was collected from 2,005 adults in the 1995 Omnibus Survey. Some results have been published in an article in *Statistical News* and 'A Household Satellite Account' (*Economic Trends,* October 1997) and in recent *Social Trends* and *Social Focus* publications. Data are deposited at the Data Archive.
Keywords: Care provided; Childcare; Housework; Leisure; Time use.

Training Statistics

ISBN: 0 11 270959 1
Publisher: The Stationery Office
Price: £18.45
Frequency: Annual
Author: Department for Education and Employment
For 1997, this publication will be combined with *Education Statistics* to produce a new publication *Education and Training Statistics in the United Kingdom.*
Keywords: Government training; Job-related training; Modern apprenticeships; Training; Youth training programme.

66 Travel Trends

ISBN: 0 11 620966 6
Publisher: The Stationery Office
Price: £30
Frequency: Annual
Author: Office for National Statistics

This annual report is a comprehensive guide to overseas travel and tourism. It provides a summary of travel patterns to and from the United Kingdom and is published in the year following the *International Passenger Survey* from which it is drawn. It illustrates how many people travel, where they go and why, and gives a picture of how long they stayed and what they spent.

Keywords: Destination of passengers; Passengers; Tourism; Transport; Travel; Visitors; Visits.

67 Women and Men in Britain 1995 - Life Cycle of Inequality

ISBN: 1 87 03 58 45 7
Publisher: Equal Opportunities Commission
Price: £12.95
Frequency: *Ad hoc* (1995)
Author: Equal Opportunities Commission

Presents statistics on topics relevant to gender equality issues based on the theme of the life cycle. Appropriate topics are shown for successive age groups, beginning with the under 16s and finishing with the over 65s. A final section contains marriage, work and earnings histories based on panel datasets.

Keywords: Birth rates; Childcare; Dependent children; Earnings; Education; Employment; Employment histories; Household and family composition; Income; Marital status; Occupation; Qualifications obtained.

Women and Men in the European Union

ISBN: 92 826 9619 7
Publisher: EUROSTAT
Price: £10.25
Frequency: *Ad hoc* (1995)
Author: EUROSTAT

This compares the situation of women and men in the European Union - how they live and work and where inequalities persist.

Keywords: Economic activity; Education; Employment; Health; Household and family composition; Immigration; Population; Social protection; Unemployment.

The Working Lives of Women and Men in Northern Ireland

ISBN: 0 90 66 46 63 4
Publisher: Equal Opportunities Commission for Northern Ireland
Price: Free
Frequency: *Ad hoc* (1993)
Author: Equal Opportunities Commission for Northern Ireland

Presents up-to-date statistics on topics relevant to gender equality issues in Northern Ireland. All tables and graphs contain gender statistics, except those concerning dependent children and household income. Comparisons are made with Great Britain.

Keywords: Benefits received; Earnings; Economic activity; Employment; Job-related training; Unemployment.

70 Youth Cohort Study

Published in the *England and Wales Youth Cohort Study Handbook: The First 10 Years*

ISBN: 0 11 27 0956 7
Publisher: The Stationery Office
Price: £29.95
Frequency: *Ad hoc* (1996)
Author: Social and Community Planning Research

This is a longitudinal survey tracking a series of cohorts of young people in England and Wales from age 16 for two years or more. To date there have been nine cohorts and the intial sample size was 20,000. The broad subject areas covered by the data include education, work, training, unemployment, qualifications and household composition.

Keywords: Absence from schools; Career provision; Earnings; Ethnic group; Job-related training; Longitudinal analysis; Qualifications obtained; School leavers; Schools; Social group; Students; Unemployment.

Section 3: Sources of further information

Sources of further information

This section suggests sources of further information about datasets or published data. Further information about particular topics or datasets is available from the contact addresses listed.

Publications

The Stationery Office or the Office for National Statistics can provide most of the government statistical publications mentioned in this *Guide* and their contact details are given below. Government departments also have their own lists of publications and can sometimes produce additional analyses on request. In addition, some key publications provide general information on sources of statistics produced by the Government Statistical Service:

Guide to Official Statistics

ISBN: 0 11 620606 3
Publisher: The Stationery Office
Price: £35.95 (also available on CD-ROM)
Date: 1996
Author: The Government Statistical Service
Contact: ONS Sales Desk (see below for details)
This is a comprehensive guide to government statistical publications.

Government Statistical Service Committee on Social Statistics Annual Report on Major Regular Social Surveys

Longitudinal Social Statistics: A Guide to Official Sources

These are free publications with brief technical information about these data sources. They are available from Deborah Scotland, Office for National Statistics. Telephone 0171 533 5788.

Electronic databases and micro-data

Many of the original datasets referred to in this *Guide* are held at the Data Archive and can be obtained for further analyses and research. The Data Archive has a comprehensive catalogue of its holdings with a topic index.

StatBase, the Government Statistical Service's forthcoming database of official statistics, is expected to become available from summer 1998 and will provide a comprehensive catalogue of the statistics produced by government, together with a route map to the statistics themselves.

Libraries

The Office for National Statistics has a comprehensive statistical library which is open to the public, as are those of the Equal Opportunities Commission and the Royal Statistical Society. Please see below for contact details.

Contact addresses for statistics

Cabinet Office - Office for Public
Service
Horse Guards Road
London SW1P 3AL
Enquiries: 0171 270 1234

Census Office for Northern
Ireland
The Arches Centre
11-13 Bloomfield Avenue
Belfast BT4 5HD
Enquiries: 01232 520 400

Data Archive
University of Essex
Colchester CO4 3SQ
Enquiries: 01206 873 333
E-mail: archive@essex.ac.uk

Department for Culture Media
and Sport
2-4 Cockspur Street
London SWY1 5DH
Enquiries: 0171 211 6000

Department for Education and
Employment
Sanctuary Buildings
Great Smith Street
London SW1P 3BT
Enquiries: 0171 925 5000

Department of the Environment
Transport and the Regions
Eland House
Bressenden Place
London SW1E 5DU
Enquiries: 0171 890 3000

Department of Health
Statistics Division
Skipton House, 80 London Road
London SE1 6LW
Enquiries: 0171 907 1000

Department of Trade and Industry
10 Victoria Street
London SW1H 0NN
Enquiries: 0171 962 8000

Department of Social Security
The Adelphi
1-11 John Adam Street
London WC2N 6HT
Enquiries 0171 962 8000

Equal Opportunities Commission
Overseas House
Quay Street
Manchester M3 3HN
Enquiries: 0161 833 9244

Equal Opportunities Commission
Northern Ireland
Chamber of Commerce House
22 Great Victoria Street
Belfast BT2 7BA
Enquiries: 01232 242752

ESRC Research Centre on Micro
Social Change in Britain
University of Essex
Wivenhoe Park
Colchester CO4 3SQ
Enquiries: 01206 872 957

EUROSTAT - Statistical Office of
the European Communities
Batiment Jean Monnet
Rue Alcide de Gasperi
Luxembourg - Kirchberg
L-2920 Luxembourg
Enquiries: 00 352 4301 1

General Register Office for
Northern Ireland
Oxford House
49-55 Chichester Street
Belfast BT1 4HL
Enquiries: 01232 252 000

General Register Office for
Scotland
Census and Population Statistics
Ladywell House
Ladywell Road
Edinburgh EH12 7TF
Enquiries: 0131 334 0380

Sources of further information

Health and Safety Executive
Statistics Division
Magdalen House
Merseyside L20 3QZ
Enquiries: 0151 951 4000

Higher Education Statistics Agency
18 Royal Crescent
Cheltenham GL50 3DA
Enquiries: 01242 255577

Home Office
50 Queen Anne's Gate
London SWH 9AT
Enquiries: 071 273 4000

Market Research Society
15 Northburgh Street
London EC1V 0AH
Enquiries: 0171 490 4911

Northern Ireland Statistics and
Research Agency
The Arches Centre
11-13 Bloomfield
Belfast BT5 5HD
Enquiries: 01232 520 400

Office for National Statistics
1 Drummond Gate
London SW1V 2QQ
General Enquiries: 0171 533 6263
Library: 0171 533 6266
Sales Desk: 0171 533 5678
Website: www.ons.gov.uk
StatBase: 0171 533 6163
NOMIS: 0171 533 6086
    e-mail: nomis-team@durham.ac.uk
Census Marketing:
Segensworth Road
Titchfield
Fareham PO15 5RR
Enquiries: 01329 813 800

Policy Studies Institute
100 Park Village East
London NW1 3SR
Enquiries: 0171 48 0468

Royal Statistical Society Library
University College of London
Gower Street
London WCE 6BT
Enquiries: 0171 387 7050 (ext 2628)

Social & Community Planning
Research
35 Northampton Square
London EC1V 0AX
Enquiries: 0171 250 1866

Social Statistics Research Unit
City University
Northampton Square
London EC1V 0HB
Enquiries: 0171 477 8000

Statistics Users' Council
Lancaster House, More Lane
Surrey, KT10 8AP
Enquiries: 01372 463 121

The Scottish Office
Education & Industry Department
Victoria Quay
Edinburgh EH6 6QQ
Enquiries: 0131 244 8400

The Stationery Office
(mail, telephone and fax orders only)
The Publication Centre
PO Box 276
London SW8 5DT
General enquiries: 0171 873 0011
Telephone orders: 0171 873 9090
Fax orders: 0171 873 8200
Counter service:
    The Stationery Office Bookshop
    59-60 Holborn Viaduct
    London EC1A 2FD

The Welsh Office
Cathay's Park
Cardiff CF1 3NQ
Enquiries: 01222 825 111

The Women's Unit
Department of Social Security
The Adelphi
1-11 John Adam Street
London WC2N 6HT
Enquiries: 0171 962 8000

Sources of further information

Section 4: Index of keywords

Index of keywords

This section cross-references the keywords with the numbered sources in Section 2 where appropriate. It is not meant to be a comprehensive index of topics covered by each data source, and is intended to complement the discussion provided in Section 1, to which it refers where appropriate.

Index of keywords

Index of keywords